The Signal of Wings

Leonie Stair

ISBN 978-1-0980-8543-8 (paperback)
ISBN 978-1-0980-8544-5 (digital)

Christian Faith Publishing, Inc.
832 Park Avenue
Meadville, PA 16335
www.christianfaithpublishing.com

Printed in the United States of America

The Signal of Wings

Look! He is coming with the clouds
Everyone shall see him
Every knee shall bow
Even those who dislike him
Never served him
Never had time for him

So shall it be
When his wings touch down
With his feet on the ground

God's Wings

God's mighty wings hover
From heaven to earth to cover those who shelter seeks
When problems arise and for his help cries
For a haven in the time of storms

A power of strength when you are weak
A generator of warmth when you are cold
A refuge when you need a hiding place
An armor from your enemies

A consolation when you are sad
A sanctuary when you want peace
A place of convalescence when you are healing
A place of love when you need a hug

Angel Wings

The wings of angels cannot hide
Unfolded and opened wide
A magnificent sight
Ready to take flight
Amid a full moon and millions of stars.

Kissed by moving clouds
Across blue skies
In the morning light
And the brilliance of the sun.

Beneath and above other planets near and far
They can reach in the blink of an eye
When commanded by God to take off.

With wings so powerful and strong
To withstand hurricanes, storms, tornados,
Gale force winds, tsunamis, and Satan
When through the heavens and earth they fly.

The Wings of Dawn

I woke up and yesterday was gone
I faced the dawn of another day
A new canvas to paint my life
To leave behind
If at the end of day, I am gone
It will be an example for all

Travel Angels

Angels in silence travel back and forth

In the night beneath the moon and stars

In the early morn at the break of dawn

In the bright sunshine to sunset time

Entering closed doors, windows, and barricades

To rescue someone that for help cries

Or to fly someone home to glory

It is the business of angels every day

Acts of Faith

Faith is the light in the dark
That Noah used to build the ark
And saved the world.

With a slingshot and a stone
David the shepherd boy, with faith,
Killed Goliath and saved a nation.

Shadrach, Meshach, and Abednego
In a fiery furnace they were thrown
Kept alive by faith, they changed a nation
From serving idols to a living God.

Gideon's weapons of clay pots and ram's horns,
By faith, defeated an army 450-1
To help a nation get to the promised land

Abraham, unwavering faith in God,
Saved his son from being sacrificed
When he passed the test of obedience
And all nations of the earth were blessed.

Joshua and his army marched without a stop
Around the walls of Jericho until it crashed
and saved a wandering nation.

Queen Ester, a woman of strong faith,
Together with Mordecai outwitted Haman
And saved the Jews in the Persian empire.

Moses faced the horrific ten plagues
And the Red sea crossing by faith
And saved a nation from further slavery.

Job the champion star of human patience
With faithfulness and allegiance
To his sovereign God won the test of trust
And got more than what in life he lost.

The thief on a cross next to Jesus
Believed him to be the son of God
And his faith in the dark got him a place in God's kingdom
Jesus sojourned on earth by faith
Preached and taught faith
Died and rose by faith
Returned to heaven by faith
Today faith abounds in the hearts of those that believe
All things are possible.

The Angel of Care

The angel of care is always near
Like a shining light
Making dull things bright

Cheering you up when your spirit is down,
Giving you faith to look up without a frown

Calming your fears
When your eyes are full of tears,

Opening doors that in your face is shut
When there is no other way in,

Pulling you up from dark pits
When you fall in and sit,

Standing behind you to protect your back
From unsuspecting attacks,

Caring for you day and night
Including fixing your plights
And winning your fights

It's the Breath of an Angel

The soft wisp of silent breeze
That gently brushes my cheeks and ruffle my hair,
It is the breath of an angel flying close to me.

Colorful petals of flowers strewn on grass and rocky paths
A beautiful mosaic,
It is the breath of an angel that scattered them

Trees in the forest, the parks, hills, valleys,
And roadsides that dance to a silent wind,
It is the breath of an angel touching them

Clouds beneath an iridescent sky forming fluffy patterns,
Large and small, freely moving aimlessly about,
It is the breath of angels having a dance

Boats propelled by a breeze
Sailing peacefully at sea,
It is the breath of angels touching their sails

Kites that fly about far up in the sky
Bringing laughter and beautiful smiles to those holding its strings,
It is the breath of angels, blowing it to and from, high and low

The Silence of Angels

Angels in silence from heaven come
To rescue those who for help cry.

Angels in silence on park benches sit
Next to lonely souls when for company they wish.

Angels in silence through closed doors walk
When children's cry of fear are heard.

Angels in silence through windows fly
When fire is blazing and someone for help cries.

Angels in silence appear on a sinking ship
When the cry for help from her captain is heard.

Angels in silence on cold frigid nights
Covers the homeless with their wings of warmth.

Angels in silence fill empty food cupboards
When the growl of hunger from stomachs are heard.

Angels in silence on a dark path appear
A shining light that dispels your fear.

Angels in silence gently relieve your aches and pain
When it is too much to bear and for relief you beg.

Angels in silence bring comfort and solace
When tears of sorrow, grief, and woes down your cheeks roll.

Angels in silence come to fly you home
When your flight to glory to them is announced.

The Lullaby

Drip, drip, drip, drip
The medicine lullaby went through her veins
Bringing slow relief from the grips of pain

Her time was near
She had lost all fear
The signal of wings she could hear

Her face lit up like sunshine
God had sent her transportation
She closed her eyes and went in peace

The angels by her side
Bore her swiftly from earth to heaven
The drip in silence left behind

If God Was Not Creative

If God was not creative,
What a dull place this world would be.

If God preferred darkness and did not create light,
What fun would there be with no moonshine, sunlight, and stars?

If God was selfish and did not create human beings of all colors that
are you and me,
A colorless race we would be.

If God was cheap and did not create angels to be transporters,
Messengers, protectors, and keepers,
Heaven would be silent and earth bereft of patron presence.

If God did not create beauty, earth would be stark and bare
Having no flowers, trees, rivers, lakes, and seas

If God did not create love,
Can you imagine?
The lack of emotion between two people
Like robots we would be.

The Leaves Had Fallen

Somewhere on the road of his life
A young man met up on hard times
He lost his job and his home
His family left him alone

The sky was his roof
The moon his light at night
The stars his chandelier
The trees his walls and shelter
The grass his carpet and bed
A stone pillow for his head

Each day alone he walked
He forgot how to talk
No longer sociable
Wandering the parks
Scurrying for food like squirrels do
In sunshine and rain

Winter came after the leaves had fallen
His carpet was covered with snow
He had nowhere to go
He stared into the sky
Opened his mouth and loudly cried,
"This is it, Lord, take me home"

God led him into a nearby church
The young man looked around
Saw a wooden cross above the altar
With Jesus looking down at him
Beneath his feet was written
"The way of the cross leads home."

The Stand

My family, friends, and comrades
This day I take a stand

I can no longer in sin dwell
Having no wish to go to hell

I met an angel in my dreams
That opened my eyes about me

I did not like what I saw
Shocked, I gave my life to God
He changed it from bad to good

Then put me on the road that leads to the promised land
Where I shall one day stand with others like myself
That made the decision to serve God

For better, not worse
For richer, not poorer
Not even in death will we part

His Angel Flowers

The elderly gentleman raised his head heavenward
The sun smiled and kissed his wrinkled face
That lit up in a great big smile

He raised his hand to touch the leaves that hung from a nearby tree
The gentle wind blew it to him instead
Bringing warmth to his cheeks

He shuffled his feet down the path to visit his wife
Beneath where his angel flowers grew
Above a beautiful headstone on which he sat down

With a sigh of contentment,
He hoped that when next to her he lay
His angel flowers' blooms will cover his headstone too

Don't Cry for Me

Do not cry for me, soft or loud
When from this earth my last breath takes me out
To be placed in a box beneath the soil
Or in a fire, burned.
My ashes placed in an urn
Where I will be but dust.
My soul alive and flown
To be with the one God I served.

Do not cry for me, soft or loud
But praise God up above
With songs and dance about
From heaven I will be looking down.

A Wonderful Feeling

What a wonderful feeling!

A very wonderful feeling!

When God's image you take on

From your head to your toes

Like a river, his love flows

Bringing joy to your soul

So much so to heaven you want to go

To thank him for this wonderful feeling

Of peace and tranquility amid life storms

Each day its mighty winds blow

Bringing golden streaks of sun

Through windows, crevices, sunroofs, and doors

The most beautiful sign that God is smiling down at us

No matter what the day brings

It is a memory to keep

If I Had Wings

If I had wings like birds that can fly

Anytime in the sky

I would go to places I want to be

Move about like a bee

Forget who I am

Avoid traffic jams,

Potholes, and crowded streets

Perch on mighty heights

Stare at all the sights,

Signs, and lights

Having no other care in the world but me

To view the world beneath my feet

Enjoying moments of peace

Within heavens reach

Left at the Altar

A woman standing at the altar
With her beautiful bouquet of flowers
No groom at her side;
He had taken off

The wonder of reasons and whys
Like bees began to buzz in her mind and head
Deep in thought besieged by grief
Tears falling to the floor
Forming a miniature pool
Reflecting a sad face of despair and hurt

An angel's wing tapped her
Speaking gently in soft tones

Be grateful it is over before it began
Good choices never change or run away
Celebrate this discovery

A Band of Holy Angels

My last sun beneath dark clouds disappeared
Like the trials I had that day

My legs were weak
My heart was racing fast
When I heard the rustle of wings

A band of holy angels coming toward me
Swooping down with graceful speed
They picked up my hands and feet

Airborne, they carried me with gentle ease
Until at heaven's door they reached

I took off my shoes
I did not need them anymore
I was about to step on golden floors with holy feet

Never Alone

Lord, thanks for keeping me company
You are the sunshine that comes in my house
Through windows, doors, crevices, cracks, and holes
From morning till sunset time

You are the shadow that before me walks
Whose footprints I step inside

It is your hand that catches me
When I am about to slip and fall

Your voice that whispers in my ears
To be at peace because you are near

It is your arms that hug me when I am sad
Your hands that wipe my eyes when my tears fall

You are the company that stays with me
When I fall asleep until the next day breaks
To greet you as we start a new day together again

Thy Will Be Done Oh! Lord

Let thy will be done oh! Lord

In my life that is yours

If you make it known to me

By angels or your holy words

I will accept it gladly as my life's occupation

Because you are the power and glory

I am your servant at thy will

The Day Will Come

My Lord! I am looking forward to the day
When I will not sit alone wishing I had company

Having no one to call my own
Only visitors who come and go

Until the day you call me home
To meet up with family and friends
Angels and other saints

One big happy family my Lord!
Forever and forevermore

The Rescue

On a very dark night
No moonshine or starlight
No dogs or stray cats in sight
The quartet left their church
Singing praises to God as they walked
On a lonely stretch of road
Toward their homes together
Dressed in long white skirts,
Blouses with sleeves to their knuckles,
Wide-brimmed hats on their head.
Bibles, God's swords in their hand
Unaware demons were nearby
Until they approached with knives drawn
Ready to rob and rape

The quartet, in hope of deliverance, began to chant,
"We are not of this world,"
"We are not of this world,"
"We are only passing through."

The demons heard the words
Frightened, they withdrew
Back into the darkness of the night

My Mountain

I came to my mountain to pray;
I was in danger of losing my crown
That I worked so hard to earn

On my knees, I cried and I cried to God
Tears flowing from the pain in my soul
In silence to the ground

Until I felt the wings of an angel
Around my shoulders, hugging me close
The whisper from the voice of God
In my heart I heard

"No more tears, my child,
I am your father in heaven
That has heard your heart's cry

Abandon your troubles at my feet
Leave it with faith and hope
Joy will follow with peace
Because I am the Lord, your God that says so."

I Come to My Garden Alone

I come to my garden alone
Full of troubles and woes
Where, in silence, my tears flow
On pebbles and stones
Rocks, brambles, dry sticks, and weeds
The picture of my life staring at me

My hands cuffed behind my back
Like a prisoner on death row
I face it all, and to God for help I cry
From the depths of my soul
Reaching up to heaven above

"Jesus, my savior and my friend,
Rescue me like Daniel from the lion's den
Get me out of this pit and set me free
Remove the plans Satan has for me
Break every chain of friction, doubt, hurt, and grief
Leave no stains in my memory of bad,
Only good let there be

"Give me a new slate to start again
That will bring joy to my heart
When in my garden I walk
With the Holy Ghost and talk
Surrounded by beautiful flowers,
Butterflies, birds, and bees."

My hands untied, free like wings
In love and peace, I shall enjoy things
I thought I had forever sacrificed
When in despair I sunk

I Am Flying

I am flying
Flying, flying, flying

I have got my holy wings
I do not need a helping hand
To glory land, I am going

I do not have one penny
Thank God, I do not need any
I can get in without money

I am flying
Flying, flying, flying
Nonstop to glory land

No turbulences or bad weather
Is forecasted for my route
To prevent my landing on heaven's runway

The Song of Angels

The angel's voices in chorus rang
From heaven to earth, singing clear and strong

Holy! Holy! Holy is our God
Holy is his name

There is none before him
None after him
He reigns eternally

Above, below, beneath this world
He alone is king

Let us adore and praise him
Our holy, holy, king
The Lord God Almighty

The Guardian

You stood by my mother's side
For nine months and watched her carry me

You were the midwife's hands that delivered me
The ever-present shadow behind me as I grew

The voice of wisdom like a gentle breeze whispering no!
When I would have yielded to Satan's will

The footprints that my feet followed
When I was unsure of where to go

The healing I felt when sick unto death
The arms that comforted me when I was sad

The wings that kept me warm when I was cold
Your sword that protected me when someone tried to harm me

The hands that lifted me when I fell so many times
The voice that praised me when I excelled in right, not wrong

The angel that beside me stands
When all is right or wrong

I Know Where I Am Going

An elderly lady sitting in her chair in her longtime home
Surrounded by things she once knew
Had no recollection of who she was,
The faces or names of friends and loved ones close
Or where she lived

A smile broke out on her face
Beside her was someone she never knew
She touched the stranger's wings
Then began to sing
Her voice loud and sweet

"Jesus, precious Jesus
My savior and friend
My day is almost done
Thank you for my angel company
Here to take me home
From a place I do not know
To a place I can never forget
My home in Glory land
On Hallelujah Avenue
You said was mine
When my life I gave to you"

"I know where I am going."

The Rustle of Mighty Wings

He held the summons with trembling hands
And read its contents;
His face turned purple,
His feet could barely stand

He thought of running to hide
But perished the thought.
The mighty rustle of wings
Belonging to God's security angels were standing guard
In front, beside, and above him

He was trapped!
Sweat trickling down his face
Contrite and subdued remorsefully begging for his life

God shook his head,
Pointed to his accountant holding his life's records
All in the red

Escorted to hell,
His screams of terror as he landed made Satan yell
"Oh! Be quiet! You worked hard for this!" as he shook his head
Making space for him in his fire pit

My Brother's Keeper

He stood in front of his brother, trembling
With the emotion coming from his aching heart
Full of guilt and remorse

With tears in his eyes and a sad tone,
He begged his brother to forgive him

"Forgive me," he said
"For pretending to be deaf
When you needed me most?"

Last night I felt the breath of air from a soft whisper
Asking, *Where is your brother?*
It was the voice of an angel
Reminding my conscience, I am your keeper

Glory! Hallelujah! Amen

Glory! Glory! Glory

It's God's Avenue
Where saints and angels walk

Hallelujah! Alleluia! Hallelujah!

It is the heavenly anthem
Praising God for everything

Holy! Holy! Holy!

Is our Lord God Almighty;
He is sacred, divine, and awesome

Amen! Amen! Amen!

From beginning to end
The Alpha and Omega
That was and is to come

The Transition

I would have been a sad story

A sad story

If Jesus from Glory had not looked my way

Saw me sway on hell's highway

Sent his angel to pull me over

That took me to a wooden cross

Where Jesus, I recognized

I gave to him my empty life

He filled it up,

Turned me around,

Placed me on solid ground,

And gave me a new route called heaven's highway

Where I now journey in the company of saints and angels

With my new best friends

Joy, a fountain of happiness

Peace, a river that never runs dry

Faith, the trusting one that keeps me strong

Hope, which I can never lose and

Love, a passion that surpasses all understanding

Redeemed

The rustle of angel's wings grew silent in heaven
The voices of those seeking forgiveness of their sins
Had reached the Shepherd's ears, always listening
for the cry of a lost sheep wanting to be found

With kindness, he claimed their souls,
Cleansing and restoring it with his seal,
Giving them a new life
Redeemed by the blood of the lamb,
The amazing love from God

When Jesus is Your Keeper

When Jesus is your keeper

A constant in your life, he is

A best friend from morn till eve

He never leaves

He watches over you

The provider of your daily bread

A guide where your feet tread

Strength when you face those you dread

The comforter when you are sad

The avenger when you have been had

The Healing Wings

A young woman laid in her bed
Struck down by an illness without a known cure,
But God, she knew
To him, she daily prayed
Until one day she gave up hope

The pain was more than she could bear
Her tears freely flowing all about
She begged God to take her out

The sound of wings, she heard
Like a mighty wind it came
Setting her free of pain that held her prisoner in her bed
Never to rear its ugly head again
She was healed

A Girl's Last Chance

Bereft from the loss of her friend,
The young girl screamed!

"Is this some cruel joke?
Did you really die?

Why! Why! Why!?"

"Your picture on my dresser
Staring back at me cannot listen
To our conversation and secrets;
It cannot hug or kiss me
Or jokingly curse at me
Neither can it walk with me to places
We loved and frequented"

"Where are you?
"I want to know?"
To heaven you surely did not go!
Because we never made time to serve God

Surprise! Surprise! Surprise!
"God gave me a last chance," replied her friend
"I am now an angel, look at me with halo and wings!"

"You look different!
"You made it into heaven!?
"Are you kidding me!?"

"No, I am not"

"Last night, just before
I took my last breath,
God gave me one last chance
To give him my heart.
In that moment, I wished
I had done it many years ago
Because the void in my life was filled;
Peace came in and covered me.
In heaven, I awoke."

"Oh my God!
"You really made it into heaven!"

Help me, Jesus!
Please! Please! Help me!
My friend has won over me
Help me, please!
You forgave her, now forgive me too!
Save my soul and fill the void within me!

God, with mercy, looked down and responded,
"I had to take your friend home
For you to realize you need me in your life.
I now forgive you, and now you are mine.

"Never again procrastinate
In a decision that concerns me,
For I am the way, the truth, and life.
I paid the price for your sins.
All you must do is acknowledge me,
Serve me,
Walk in my light,
Do right, and never lose sight of who I am."

In Our House

In our house is our home
A place where family is fully defined
And it is understood
That God is the head whom our family serves

No weapon formed against it shall be drawn
No curses can enter,
Linger, or be accommodated

Nor the power of evil prosper
Because the mighty power of God
Cleanses all unrighteousness inside out

For he is our king
Whose angels protect and keep us safe
From all harm and dangers

In our home, where we will always
welcome those who enter
Its atmosphere of love and warmth

Lost Angel Wings

Burning heat, she felt above the ground
She was floating around
In a dark place that felt quite strange

A light from above shone in her face
Startled! She looked up and saw people
Flying happily in God's space

Aghast! Frightened! She looked down,
Beneath her was a burning furnace
With Satan's face staring back at her

She now knew for sure she was not safe
Going downward into a place
She never envisioned to one day face

Fear gripped her heart
She shouted, "Help! Help! I need help!
God Almighty, I need help!"

She pulled out her iPhone to dial 911
It was a blob of plastic and metal;
The heat had melted it

In full-panic mode, she screamed!
"God, help me, please! Please!
This is not a cool breeze; it is burning heat!"

Satan giggled and laughed out loud
She could hear him clearly up close
While God far above shouted to her!

"I gave you your life,
With the opportunity to give me your heart
But you were too busy tearing lives apart

With your gossip and strife.
You destroyed your wings for heaven;
Your room has been taken."

She awoke, gasping for fresh air,
Sweat pouring off her body
Down on her knees
Praying to God for a clean heart

Mama! Mama!

"Mama! Mama!
I am searching for you
Where in heaven are you?"

"I have looked in every nook and cranny,
Believing that when you took an early flight,
Heaven your destination would be.
But I see something went wrong,
Nowhere in heaven can you be found."

"Dear child, stop searching for me up there.
I booked the wrong flight;
It landed me in a hot spot
Where there are no outgoing flights."

"Mama! Mama!
That is hell and a big mistake
That cannot be fixed."

"I know! I know, my child!
I should have paid attention
And made the right decision
To avoid this destination."

It Would Have Been a Sad Story

It would have been a sad story
If Jesus did not come to earth from glory,
A promise would have been broken
With no redemption for sinful man
If Satan had conquered him
And cancelled the crucifixion

If he had come as a royal subject,
The poor would not have met him
Or behind him thronged
To witness his sayings and holy work

If he did not have disciples and media
To document his life on earth,
His story would not be told

If he had returned to Glory
When vilely and cruelly treated
Before they hung him on a cross
And from the dead he had not risen,
There would be no ascension
Or the day of Pentecost and the Holy Ghost

Don't Cry for Me, Mama

Do not cry for me, Mama!
You taught me right from wrong,
God's way, his truth and life
That took me through heaven's gates

Do not cry for me, Mama!
I know you miss me too,
But here in heaven, I am no longer
Crippled, or wheelchair-pushed
I am free of pain and suffering
I walk, skip, and fly with angels
Throughout heaven's golden courts

Do not cry for me, Mama!
Heaven is a happy place
With family, friends, angels
Prophets, kings, and holy saints

Do not cry for me, Mama!
God's face I see every day
Before his throne I stand
Happily praising him

Do not cry for me, Mama!
I will meet you at heaven's holy gates
When with joy you step inside
Never ever to part company with me again

The Great Fall

I knew right from wrong
Attended church on Sabbath days
Heard the prayers of those who for me prayed
Laughed out loud when there was altar call
Ignored it all

Thinking the Christian path was dull
Until my fate I met when I had a great fall
That changed my mind

Now full of regrets
That the sins of my flesh
Took control and sentenced me

I had no one to call
I had walked out on those who cared
Without once looking back

I went to the deep river's edge
Thinking all was lost
Ready to kiss the earth goodbye

When I heard wings;
A mighty angel shoved me backwards
Into the path that led me to calvary
Where I met Jesus and gave my heart
For a new life on a clean path

Seven Day Invites

Monday, someone knocked on a young woman's door
With an invite to meet Jesus,

She rolled her eyes and replied,
"I have better things to do,
Give it to someone else."

Tuesday, an old lady gave her a poster
"Jesus is coming soon," it read

"Yeah! That is a joke," she smirked
She threw it in the recycle bin

Wednesday, her neighbors voice
Singing, "Jesus is the answer," reached her ears

Disgusted, she put on her headphones,
Grumbling as she did
"I have no time for her crowing
Nor an answer to a question."

Thursday, her best friend called,
"Aye, I found Jesus.
I want to tell you about it."

"Oh! No, you do not.
You must be crazy,
What got into you?"
"Jesus, and you need him too."

"Really!? I do not think so,
I am doing fine.
Bye! I have work to do."

Friday, a message was left on her desk
From a co-worker,
"Prayer meeting tonight at my home.
Join me; there is much to give God thanks for."

She sent her back a reply,
"I do not need company to give thanks,
I am too busy anyway."

Saturday, her father called her
"Hi, honey, let's go to church tomorrow,"

"Sorry, Dad, it's the only day I have for myself
I can't give it up."

Sunday, Jesus came to call
She could not close her door
Or turn him down

Marcia Dorrett Clarke-Hinton
October 30, 1960 — December 30, 2010

Fly, Fly, to Glory Land

Goodbye, goodbye, my best friend
Fly, fly, and fly to glory land
You have earned your angel wings
A star-jeweled crown and seat around God's throne

We, down here from where you have flown,
Walk in a stupor with a frown,
Temporarily enraged,
Unable to comprehend
Your unexpected leave without a word,
A kiss,
A hug, or a handshake

Even though we understand
When death calls, you must go
Leaving behind friends and loved ones
Trying to be brave

Teardrops falling on our cheeks
As we weep and lose sleep
Grieving the absence of a mother so rare
A daughter so special and dear

A granddaughter so worthy and special
A church member so loving and kind

An aunt so understanding and warm
A cousin so dependable and cool

A niece so caring and witty
A sister every sibling adores

A coworker with integrity and grit
A friend closer than a brother or sister

Leaving behind good memories so sweet
To be kept as keepsakes until again we meet
(In loving memory of my friend Marcia Hinton who died in a tragic
accident in December 2011.)

The Messengers of Heaven

Angels are always around
In the old and new testaments
A record of their visits is told;
They never cease to come and go

Like the angel Gabriel,
Messenger of wisdom and special events

To Daniel he appeared
When his visions needed sorting out

Many years later to Zacharias
He bore the good news
His barren wife a son would birth
To prepare the way for God's only son

To be birthed by a virgin girl named Mary
Whom he told the good news
That she was chosen to carry the Christ child
That shall save his people from their sins

To Joseph, her fiancé, in a dream he appeared
To bring understanding of his privileged obligation
To the chosen mother of the Christ child

Angel Sunrise

Sunshine smiles,
Hugs, and kisses
Hands waving
See you later
Start the little angel's day
On a cold December day, 2012
In Connecticut, USA

Safety unquestioned
A daily routine
Not expecting
The unexpected rush of an angry ferocious wind
A violent prey—insane, selfish,
No longer humane
Digits pressing
Metallic arrows
Furious fire sprays
Like lightning
Shatters the pitter-patter of little feet
In their school

Innocent targets
Frightened
Momentous screams

A nation weeps!

Seconds,
Minutes
Twenty little children's feet
Enter through heaven's door,
Converge on holy grounds

No family around them stood
A broken circle...
Angels by their side

Sudden silence!

Cherub faces crumple
Tears falling on golden floor

The King of heaven close to them stood,
Gently to them spoke

"No tears in heaven, my little angels,
Give it all to me."

"Climb in my arms
This is your new home
No harm
No fear
No pain
In my heaven can be found."

Wings of Rescue

The young woman put her books away
She was tired and laid down to sleep
Under God's keep
To wake the next day
Full of plans to complete

She drove her car on a busy street
A careless driver crashed her into the divider
And did not stop

She walked out of the wrecked car, unhurt
Thanking God for saving her
As she watched her crumpled car lifted onto a wrecker

Not securely fastened,
It slid down toward her,
A sure death if unseen hands
Had not picked her up
Moved her out of harm's way

It was an angel standing guard,
The holy wings of rescue

Bone Cold

The homeless woman
Sat on a very cold stone,
Shivering and alone

She had no winter coat
To keep her warm

Each day she prayed to God
For summer to bump the winter
To ease her woe

Bone cold,
She looked up at houses aglow,
Smoke spiraling in the cold night air
Coming from the chimneys

She whispered from her heart,
"I wish I had a family
And a home with a warm hearth."

God heard her desire
Sent his angel with the warmest wings
To bring her swiftly home

A Free Ticket to Glory Land

I had gone everywhere
Except to heaven land
Because I was never interested
If ever such a place existed
To find out where it was

I walked by a holy chapel one early morning
Advertising on their bulletin
Were "Free tickets to heaven land,
Come on in and get one."

The message grabbed my interest;
I went right in through an open door

I did not see anyone around
Disappointed, I turned to leave
When I heard the flapping of wings

I looked up expecting to see a misguided bird
When my eyes saw a note
Tacked upon a wooden cross that read

"I am your free ticket to heaven land.
I paid for it at Mount Calvary.
Accept it gladly with all your heart."

Touched by the generosity,
I humbly accepted the gift
A free ticket I held in my hand
To heaven land

Angels Everywhere

Angels, like winds they appear
Where they are sent
Any day and anytime

Sitting in a pew,
Lounging on a park bench,
Hanging out in your house

On a trip
Next to you in an airplane,
Sailing on a ship,
Or sitting under a tree

Angels, visible and invisible
You cannot keep them away
When God sends them your way
Anywhere and everywhere

Heaven's Walkway

The sun was setting,
Her walk was almost done
She looked behind her,
Saw the distance she had come

The trials and good times now far behind
She was headed for heaven land

The sounds of rustling wings
She heard was close
A sign she was almost there

In preparation, she dusted off her feet
Shouting as she did
"Holy One, here I come."

Heaven's walkway lit up,
Guiding her to heaven's door
With Jesus standing waiting

Hands outstretched with a golden crown
He placed upon her head
To welcome her home

Little Children

Little children, little children
God's awesome jewels
Like sunshine in the skies
They brightly shine each day

Little children, little children
God's little angels
Shining in their beauty
In God's holy kingdom

Little children, little children
God's little blessings
Pure and holy at his feet they sit

Little children, little children
God's crowning glory
Like gems, they surround him

Little children, little children
No matter their story
Always have a place in glory

Cracked Up

An angel of rescue
I stood above a crack pit

I could hear the boy shuffling,
Sniffling, and slip sliding
Among skeletons all cracked up

Someone had called
To bring him home

My master heard,
Sent me to get him

I called his name,
A voice he did not recognize
I called him again, again, and again

I tried to reach him,
But he slipped back in many times
Unwilling to grab my outstretched hand

Unrelenting, I kept up the beat,
Encouraging him to make the first move
Finally, tired and cracked up,
He reached for my hand
I pulled him out

New life to him, I delivered
From the King of kings

His reaction of praise
Through the streets rang
"Thank God for cracking down on me."

Angel Rescue

God, you know my story
Before I was born
The one told to me
So many times about how
My daddy left my mommy
In front of a health clinic,
Her bill prepaid

Scared and alone,
She stepped up to the clinic door
When a mighty rustling sound she heard
Coming toward her

Frightened and afraid,
with haste she ran down the streets
Back to her house to her seven children
Cuddled under the wings of an angel
God sent to rescue us

With tears streaming down her face
For nine months, she carried me
Through good and bad times
With God in her life

She taught me right from wrong:
To serve you all the time,
How to love, and how to be kind

A successful rescue, I am
Owing it all to you, for that day
My mama ran scared
From the rustling she heard
Coming from the wings
Of an angel you sent to rescue me

The More He Climbed

Educated, healthy, financially stable
This young man thought he had everything
He was moving upward with his skills
Not caring that God was the power
And glory behind everything

The more he climbed
The more ground the devil gained
Until God stepped away, and he had a great fall

The breath of an angel woke him up
His eyes opened wide
Glad to be alive and able to move

He got on his knees and, to God, prayed
To change his life and walk with him

Each step he now takes is never without God
That is his power and glory

A Mother's Dream

My son,
Last night I dreamed that
God's great judgment day had come
To heaven I was flown
Where you could not be found

I stood with other mothers
Also missing sons
The angels pointed to your records
Of the times you all turned Jesus down,
Too busy having fun

Brokenhearted, we clung to each other,
Knowing your faces we would never again see
Tears of grief from our eyes sprung
When God's angels in unison spoke,

"No tears or grief in heaven is allowed,
Your sons grew no wings,
There is naught you can do now."

My son, let not this dream be a reality
I do not want to search heaven in vain for you.

I Hear My Angel Wings

The night was dark,
No moon was shining,
No stars were out
The homeless man laid on the park bench
His stench rose in the light breeze blowing
Ruffling his ragged dirty garments

He was hungry
His belly was groaning
His eyes were slowly closing
When he heard a rustling sound
Coming from a nearby tree

He whispered softly to the air,
"My bench will soon be empty
The garbage bins unruffled
My dirty garments discarded
I am going home to glory
My angel wings are hovering."

The Sidewalk Beggar

The man in tattered garments stood
On the busy metro sidewalk
His hand outstretched, a-begging

Many people passed him without a glance
Some shook their heads in scorn,
Others shooed him out of their path

An old lady gave him a dollar,
A soldier removed his coat
And covered his shivering body

A teenage boy pulled off his wool hat,
Placed it upon his cold head,
Smiled, and went on his way

A little girl waved and smiled at him
That was all she had to give

A street vendor gave him a hotdog,
A cup of coffee, and a packet of ketchup

The beggar's test of human kindness completed
He shed his disguise and opened his wings

Covering those to him kindness showed
With blessings for a lifetime

Faith, Joy, Hope, Peace

Lord, when my faith is weak,
Let me humbly to you speak
To cover me with thy grace
Not to let me fall in disgrace

When no joy I feel,
Let me on my knees kneel
To ask you once again to fill me up
Not to let me sit and mope in an empty cup

When I lose hope,
Let my hands and feet not grope
In darkness and defeat
But grab faith to give hope back to me

When peace in my heart is disturbed
By demons that around me lurk,
Let me not sink in despair
But with hope and faith dispel the fear
To bring peace back my way

The Council

Congregated in glory were Peter, James, and John
Matthew, Mark, and Luke
Phillip, Andrew, and Jude
Paul, Timothy, and Titus
Thomas, Stephen, Elijah, and Elisha
Looking down on earth

What they saw made them wonder
What on earth was happening!
They saw the devil on a roll
Snuffing out the beatitudes,
Filling the world with a false beat of love

A religious financial kingdom
Where Jesus is used for a moneymaker
Not acclaimed as King, but a hero like human beings

In sadness, they searched the world
Hoping to see many Holy Ghost-filled preachers,
Healers, and teachers in Jesus's name
A revival of faith, truth, and saving grace
In nook and corners everywhere

They saw instead feebly Christians praying,
Struggling to stand firm in their faith
With one foot in and one foot out

Elijah and Elisha in unison spoke,
"They are losing their wings, my brothers,"
"A true signal," remarked Titus

Saint Paul shook his head and said,
"John, your revelation is happening.
Jesus must be on the brink of visiting them soon."

Heaven's Path

Heaven's path begins with the cross
With salvation in your heart

If your mind is made up to walk it right,
Obey the signs and be courageous

Ignore the devil that will appear anytime
Trying to trip you to weaken and fall

Let faith and hope keep you strong
Never let God out of your sight

There is no telling what you will meet
That will keep you forever out of heaven's reach

The Power of Prayer

When the Holy Ghost in your life exists,
The power of prayer is a mighty tower
To be used if you genuinely believe
God answers prayer, making all things possible

He can move mountains out of your life,
Make crooked paths straight,
Divide red seas for you to cross
He can let demons flee from out of your way,
Calm and still the waves of any storm
That can blow you away into deep waters
He can raise your faith to spiritual heights
To experience a holy ride above high tide
He can open your blind eyes
To see his footsteps to step inside
When caught in places you need an out
He can open your deaf ears to his holy words
To make sound decisions
When you are at a crossroad
He can heal your body, soul, and spirit
What ever is your diagnosis, he has the cure
Praying is heaven's apothecary
Having a remedy for all things
When with faith we believe all things are possible

The Whisper of an Orphan Girl

Forlorn and alone
In the early morn,
An orphan girl on a river's bank sat
On a large moss-covered stone

Staring at the river speckled with ducks
And their ducklings having early morning fun,
Bringing back memories of her parents
That once surrounded her with love

She whispered softly, "Why, Lord? Why, my Lord?
Why did you take them from me?
Why did they leave me all alone?
My living is so ho-hum."

Rivulets of teardrops flowed down her cheeks
As she wept and hugged herself to keep warm

The sun burst forth in brilliant sunlight
Its hot rays shining down on her

Birds from their perch in trees
Flew down and converged at her feet
Singing tweet, tweet, tweet

Rabbits hopped over in a frolic
As a wandering pup climbed in her lap
Yapping at her playfully

A slight wind rose, swaying branches,
Dropping ripe fruits to the ground
She happily gathered them to eat
Enjoying the love God sent her way

Amen

Amen! Amen! Amen!
So be it; it is so
Angels in glory, shout it out

Amen! Amen! Amen!
So be it; it is so
Believers in Christ say it over and over

Amen! Amen! Amen!
So be it; it is so
When to God we pray

Amen! Amen! Amen!
So be it; it is so
When to God our life is given

Amen! Amen! Amen!
So be it; it is so
When to heaven we go

Leap for Life

Everything is not all right
When the devil has you doing wrong,
Hugging you to him all day long
On his warm cozy chest
To put you to the test
To be his friend
In darkness, where he lives
Above a bottomless pit
Filling up with those he tricks

Listen to a wise tip
Take a leap into God's way
His angels are always on duty
That will catch you when you do

The Dawn of a New Day

Each day I rise from my sleep in the night
To behold the dawn of a new day
Filled with sunlight, snow, or frigid cold
Scorching heat, rain, or stormy winds
I give God thanks for it with grateful praise

He could have taken me home
At any time during the night

To leave behind family for whom I care,
Friends with whom I share happy times
To grieve and mourn my demise

No matter what the new day brings
I will not complain or wear a frown
Being alive to experience it
Makes me grateful to love, laugh, and live
One more day in God's world

The Color Blend

More beautiful than the rainbow

Or anything I know

Around God's throne, in a circle

Amazing faces

Of all races,

Angels and spirits

Holding hands together with God

A colorful blend;

One people under God

Riding Heaven's Clouds

Stress and distress from our lives;
We will no more endure
When Jesus calls us to come home

With a smile, we will go,
Riding on clouds that will never sway,
Touching down on heaven's runway

Lined on each side with angels
Waiting to escort us through heaven's gateway
To meet our King,
At whose feet we shall humbly fall
Thanking him for taking us in

This Is His Story

It was morning light,
Bright and sunny
The young man, fully awake,
Was not impressed by morning glory
It made no difference
If there was sunlight or night;
He was depressed

The time had come to end it all
He went outside
A rope coiled in his hands
He visited a tree
Just the right height
Preparing the rope to size

The task completed
He stood on a stone to reach
A branch to do the job
When he heard the rustle of wings
Startled, he fell to the ground

A gentle hand reached out to him
Lifting him up to stand on his feet

It was the hand of a loving God
That saved him from self-destruction
Giving him a chance
To lay his problems at his feet
To be rid of self-defeat

The Broken Grip

His body scarred,
Teeth decayed and stinking breath,
Hair knotted in a thousand threads
Sporting pebbles, grass, and tree buds

Below his brow his eyes looked out
Of sunken sockets, unfocused
His face gripped in his palms
Shedding tears of regrets
When he remembered God's love

He got on his knees and prayed
Down in the gutter
A place he feared no one would come

But God heard his cry
Sent his angel to break the devil's grip
And set him free

The Journey

I started this journey
From earth to heaven
When Jesus I met and gave him my heart
I had a rough start, but it never stopped me

When so many crossroads I met in my path
With the devil grinning on the side
Hoping on the wrong road I would slide

But God, my shining light,
Shone on the road I should take
Safe out of the devil's path
Angels guiding me

Thank you, God, for being at my crossroads
I have learned them by heart and sight
All written in your Holy Book

The Ride

The headstrong boy went on a ride
With demons as his guide,
Wreaking havoc day and night
Hurting anyone in his path
Was his way of life

Until one day he heard wings
That stopped him in his act
It was the hands of the almighty God
Reaching for his heart

He gave it all to him
The frightened demons took flight
Leaving him featherlight
To serve God that saved his soul

God's Creation of Life

God's creation of life is everywhere
In darkness and in the light
Beneath the stars, the moon at night,
And the sun that brings daylight

On mountain tops,
In the valleys,
On the plains,
Beneath the seas, lakes, and rivers

In the wilds,
In the zoo,
In the air;
Everywhere life is found

Where angels, people, and animals
On earth and in heaven are found
That breathes and moves.

When Snow Falls

Come winter, snowfall is often a welcome sight
By those who enjoy the fluffy white crystal flakes
That settle on the ground, rivers, and lakes
Like a crinoline; it hangs onto evergreens
Plants, houses, and trees
Covers forests, hills, and mountains
Fills up holes and containers

Some shaped like the wings of angels
Creating a breathtaking beauty
Of nature's spotless purity
That will last until it is melted
To return when forecasted or unexpectedly
If winter lasts

When untouched upon the ground,
An example of when God's blood cleansed us
Drawing attention to God's beauty in us

Any Time, Any Day

The devil is a power of frustration
Turning up everywhere
Any time of any day
That is his play date
Hoping you will curse
When stumbling upon blocks he puts in your path

But God's angel next to you
Secure your hands and close your mouth
When with violence you are tempted to retaliate
When the devil is laughing in your face

The Knock

Each day there is a knock on a door
In our house
In offices
Anywhere there is a door

We respond if we want to
But there is one knock
Man does not always hear
Because it is different
From the sound on a wooden,
Metal, or glass door

It is the knock of an angel
On your heart's door
The only way into your soul
That God wishes to enter in

Listen for this special knock
You never want to miss it
He may not knock again

By His Power, We Are Fed

Every day that God sends
Some tables are bountifully spread
Others have only bread
While there are those who go to bed
With hungry bellies not fed

To them God sends
His angels of kindness
Like the widow's mite
By his power, they are fed

Saved by Prayer

My brother,
Healthy and strong,
Doing no known wrong,
Helping the needy,
Being a good friend,
Father, brother, son, and uncle,
Going to church,
Serving God the way he knows how

When the devil
Vexed inside out
Because he had lost him to good works

Surprising everyone,
He struck him down
In a coma like he was dead
In a hospital bed

His organs were on go slow
Angels were flying low
The devil, with his feet cocked up,
Was anticipating a grand celebration
When he finally would take him out

Ignoring the fact that God is not deaf
When prayers from voices far and near
Like hail rained on heaven's door

God commanded the angel of death to stand still
A miracle was happening;
He was about to answer some prayers

My brother, out of his coma, awoke
Full recovery with time
A medical wonder
But to us it is the evidence of the power of God
To heal and restore health when we ask

The Sound

I woke to a sound I had never heard before
Loud enough to wake the dead and open the ears of the deaf
I jumped out of bed and ran outside

There were people everywhere!
How did they get here? I wondered!
Some in pajamas like I was
Many in formal and informal wear
Others walking around naked and in a daze

Cellphones! iPhones! iPods! A dismal sight
Abandoned like garbage piled high on the ground
Forming mountains around the crowd
No talking, no texting, no emailing, no Instagram
No Twitter, no Skype, no picture taking, no Google search

They were all staring up into the clouds
I too looked and saw a bright shining angel
That stood with one foot on land and the other on the sea

I wondered if I was dreaming but snapped out of it
When the angel raised his hands toward heaven
Declaring, "Time is no longer to be."

He opened a book and began calling names
Not every family members or friend's name was in it

Heartrending cries ensued from mothers,
Fathers, sisters, brothers, children, cousins,
Sweethearts, and friends bent in grief

Some of the rich and mighty
Like paupers they stood
No money could get their names in the book
No matter how they pleaded

Great men abandoned cried like babies
When their greatness made no difference
Like regular persons, they joined the doomed
Begging the rocks and mountains to fall on them

Shaking, I stood covered in cold sweat
Wondering if my name would be called

The Upper Room

Apostles, believers, men, and women,
Obediently to the upper room they went
Together they began to pray
With sincerity and faith

Jesus, in heaven, heard them clearly
His promise he fulfilled that hour
Called the day of Pentecost

Like a mighty host of angel wings
The Holy Ghost, like a ferocious wind,
Upon them descended
Taking control of their tongues
To speak languages they never spoke before

With gifts to heal the sick
The power of prophecies
To a world in ignorance
Of salvation and Christianity

Pentecost continues to this day
When, with faith, we empty our hearts
To accept the Holy Ghost
That keeps us safe and sound
In mind and spirit to do our part
According to what God gifted us

Burnt Wings

Satan, you fallen angel
Move out of my way
You are trouble
I do not want your company

We are not friends
You are my enemy
Your disguise cannot fool me

For God is my father
He is the conqueror,
The mighty lion of Judah
You cannot touch me

My father, Jesus's blood, circles me
Do not ever try to get in
Go back to the pit of hell
Spend some time to get familiar with it

Soon, and very soon,
Jesus is going to lock you in it
Where you cannot fly, swim, or slither out

What a deliverance day that will be
To the shout of victory
From those whom you could not deceive

As they witness your agony and loss of power
When your wings are burnt to cinders
Your freedom forever gone

Jesus, Precious Jesus

Jesus, precious Jesus
A royal king in a stable born
God's only child

In the river of Jordan was baptized
Setting the pace for others to follow

On Mount Calvary, he died
On the third day, he arose
The price of sin was paid;
To heaven, he ascended

Jesus, precious Jesus
To us so much he has given
Our savior and our God

To earth he will one day come again
To separate the good from the bad

Jesus, precious Jesus
The sweetest name in heaven and earth
Around whom all angels stand,
Praising him all day long

Sister Gossip

Sister Gossip walked into church
Never late, always on time
Watching everyone within her view

She could not wait for the end of
"Praise God from whom all blessings flow,"
Before she grabbed church members
Willing to listen to her criticize…

Sister Mary who was on public assistance,
Brother John praying for a wife,
Deacon Paul who could barely read and write,
Young Elijah with the crush on Sister Pearl,
Little Faith who had no job,
Sister Norma whose husband left her

The church members
Accommodated her with a fake smile
Until one Sunday, after morning service,
Old mother Zion cornered her
Held the Holy Bible to her chest
Rebuked her in Jesus's name

An angel covered Sister Gossip's mouth
Not a word from it came out
The Holy Ghost had shut her up

Jesus Is a Forever Friend

Jesus is a forever friend
When in his image you walk

In good times and bad times,
He never walks away

When things get dim or dark,
He surrounds you with brightness

If you lose your way,
He guides you back with hope

If you are sad and tearful,
He dries your tears with faith

When you are afraid,
His angels surround you

If you are lonely,
He sends you joy for company

You never have to worry;
He is your forever friend

The Call

There is one city that I cannot go
Until I am told it is time

When, to this city, I am called
It is a journey I will enjoy

Taking a ride through the skies
Guided by angels to the city of gold to reside

What a wonderful day that will be
To be met by a king so kind

Waiting for me to arrive
To wear the crown he has for me

One I earned with patience and faith
Never betraying or ignoring him

Who Is Satan?

The devil is a deceiver
A Leviathan serpent and Satan
Angel of the bottomless pit
On a crusade with his band of demon angels
Trying to deceive the vulnerable and weak

Like a lion, the king of beasts,
He walks about seeking
Those whom he can devour,
Transforming himself into an angel of light

For he has the power to be just what he wants
Once an anointed covering cherub,
He wanted to be equal to God
A rebellion in heaven he started,
But to earth, a fallen star, he came

A son of perdition, Lucifer, and the little horn
The King of Tyre, Beelzebub,
Dragon, Belial, Beast, and Antichrist;
Aliases by which he is known and called

Only the blood of Jesus
The seal of God on your body, soul, and spirit
Can withstand the power he wields

His time of reign is short,
Seeking ways and means to capture souls
Before he is bound by an angel

Sealed in a bottomless pit
For a thousand years
After that to be loosed, a little season

To deceive people once again
Too deaf and blind to his tricks
Until he and them is cast into a lake of burning fire
With brimstone and false prophets

The Train in a Frolic

The happy train made many stops
Encouraging everyone to hop on
No one bothered to look at the sign
That read, "Hell-bound express"

The moment they got in,
It speeded along,
Picking up people all day long

The devil was the engineer,
Whistling as he guided the train
On hell's train track

The passengers of all races
The rich and the poor
Altogether enjoying the tour

Until someone shrieked,
"There are skeletons under our seats
All burned from head to feet."

Everyone looked!
Together they shouted to Satan,
"Stop the train!"
Begging to get off

Satan shouted back to them!
"Remain in your seats everyone.
I did not force you to take this ride
To hell, we are going; it was your choice"

Hotter and hotter the temperature rose
Louder and louder the devil laughed
When the people tried to get off

He made a final stop at the mouth of a pit
Where he pitched them headlong into it
In vain, they screamed to God for help

He shook his head; they were on their own
They had many times turned him down
Too late for them to turn around

Some Days We Wish for Wings

Some days we wish for wings
To fly us far from earth
With its problems everywhere
Like a live volcano
Shooting hot and burning lava
Each way we turn

Sometimes we even wonder
Where is our God?
When it seems hope is lost

A plea from our hearts,
From the frustrations we feel,
His presence in silence appears

To quickly still the storms and put out our fires
To calm our fears and dry our tears
Letting us know he is still in charge of this world
Filled with problems and woes
Created by Satan and his folks

The Door Closed

The trumpet sounded,
The dead responded,
The living heard it,
The world's activities ceased;
Time mattered no more

Angels, like the sand of the sea,
Gathered around all nations,
Standing in front of God,
Listening for their names

He looked at their records
Beckoned the faithful
Through heaven's door

He closed the books
Without a backward glance,
He followed behind

Astonished, the people abandoned
Observe heaven's gates silently close

They looked around for another door
And met upon Satan cowering,
Searching for a place to hide,
Screaming to God to save him

The crowd joined in
No answer came back

They ran rampant and wild
Trying to take their lives,
But suicide was not a choice
Death was on hold
Hell was heating up

Too late,
Roll call had ended

The Great Celebration

The great judgment day roll call was ended
Those whose name in the Lamb's book of life
Behind the Lamb of God, they followed;
Together they rose, and through the sky
To heaven's runway, they arrived

Stripped of their earthly clothes and shoes,
Wearing heavenly garments
Behind the Lamb for sinners slain, they walked through heaven's
gates

From all the corners of heaven
Loved ones, friends, apostles came
Greeting the new arrivals with heaven's love

Together they walked into heaven's ballroom
Prepared for a celebration never in heaven before seen
The holy orchestra surrounded by heaven's choir of angels
Children of all ages around God's kingdom sat

The brilliance of God lit heaven up
There was no need of any other light
Not the sun, moon, or stars

From every voice burst forth praises to God and the Lamb
The orchestra and musicians of every instrument in God's heaven
Began to play as heaven's choir began to sing

Holy! Holy! Holy is our Lord Almighty!
Holy! Holy! Holy is our Lamb!
He has conquered death and hell and rid his world of Satan

Glory! Glory! Glory! Glory!
To our God Almighty,
Our Father who art in heaven
Holy is his name

Amen! Amen! Amen!
It is joy unmatched and full of glory

The alpha and omega,
The beginning and end

Angel Lullaby

Two little boys
Curled up together like two little kittens
Under their comforter
Listening to their drunken father
Stumbling and falling,
Cursing and arguing with their mother

Beneath the covers, they held hands
Praying to Jesus to let him stop
Suddenly everything went quiet
Except for the sound of someone singing

The eldest boy whispered,
"Do you hear singing?"

"Yes," replied the younger child
"It is the angel lullaby.
God has sent us angel company.
We can go to sleep now."

Never Give Up

When to God you give back your life
It is the start of a very new living
Your ways of yesterday are no more
Your days of today are now heaven bound

Journeying in the company of saints
Protected by angels and the Holy Ghost
That will guide you into the Christian paths
That the devil may try to block
To test your faith in God

Never give up
Keep your eyes upon the cross
Where Jesus died for you
Look at the nails in his hands and feet
It is enough to keep you on his street

172 | LEONIE STAIR

Give Thanks

We get up in the morning
On earth that is the Lord's
Full of the beauty of creation
From the sky to the ground
All around us, a witness of God's love

The birds that sing perched on trees,
Flowers that bloom in many colors
Gulls above the sea that dive within its depths,
A water world of beauty and living things;
Its waves in crystal splendor rise and to the shore dies

Trees that, in their colorful splendor, are everywhere
Some laden with fruits or nuts to eat or just leaves for shade
Mountains, valleys, glaciers, canyon, oceans, falls, and reefs
We see and enjoy each day we rise and, in this world, live
Protected by God and his angels
Let us give thanks

I Am Blessed

I get up in the morning
I am breathing;
I am blessed

The sun is shining
A new day has begun;
I am blessed

Rain is falling
A roof is over my head;
I am blessed

Food on my table
I will not go hungry;
I am blessed

Clothes on my body
I will not be naked;
I am blessed

Shoes on my feet
I will not be bare feet;
I am blessed

Money in my bag
My finances intact;
I am blessed

I can hear
I can speak;
I am blessed

Angels guarding me
I am safe;
I am blessed

I have Jesus
He made all this possible;
I am blessed

King of the World

God is the King of heaven and earth
From beginning to end

He rules the world with majesty and power
No other ever can

He is the conqueror of death and hell,
The giver and protector of life

Exalted he stands before his throne
Before him, all nations must bow

The King of kings
The Lord of lords

He alone is God
The creator of all mankind

I Shall Rise

I shall rise
From beneath the soil
Where I was buried when I died

I shall rise
From out of urns, canisters, and jars
Where my ashes were stored

I shall rise
When my ashes come together
From where it was scattered

I shall rise
Out of the guts of scavengers
From beneath the sea, in rivers, and wells

Where I died

I shall rise
From the dust of the ground
Where I was burned to cinders

I shall rise
From everywhere I was laid
When death took me out

I shall rise
To receive my just reward
From God up above

When his holy trumpet sounds
The signal to the dead and living
That heaven's roll call is about to begin

Silence in the City

I woke up one morning thinking everything was fine
Until I realized it was just too quiet in a city that never sleeps

No sirens from police cars, ambulances, or fire trucks!

No one banging on walls or slamming doors!

No garbage trucks noisily throwing down garbage bins!

No children screaming, nor babies crying!

No couples loudly arguing!

No phones ringing!

No TV or radio sounds!

No yellow cabs screeching to a stop!

No Uber, Lyfts, or gypsy cabs pulling up at curb sides!

No one walking around!

Everyone and everything at a stand still
Just too quiet to make sense to me

Until I looked up into the sky
Beheld the King of glory in all his splendor
Surrounded by countless angels
Descending from heaven, a glorious sight

A New Start

When from sin you turn,
A new life begins
With Jesus Christ as your King

Whom you must trust
With your entire being

If you walk, you will not fall
He gives you strength to keep on moving

If you run, you will not faint
His blood is enough to keep you strong

When you are thirsty, you will not dehydrate
He is the water of life

When you testify of his amazing saving grace,
You will do it with confidence from your heart

When to heaven you are called,
Your wings you earned will open,
Ready for takeoff

God Is Real

There are many things I may not know
But one thing is for sure: I know God is real

He is everywhere and can be seen looking down
In the sunshine, moon, and stars

The awe! Of wonder in the beauty of the world we see
Springing up from the soil in beautiful plants and flowers

The change of seasons: Spring, Summer, Autumn, and Winter
The sea, lakes, rivers, and waterfalls that never run dry

The miracle of birth which no other can perform
The brilliance of man's mind to think, do, and make

The sound of thunder that shatters in the air
And lightning that strikes in the rain

Night and day that alternates
Angels that come and go

The feeling in our hearts and soul
When God is our control
We attest he is forever real

My Girl

This day was special for this mother,
With tears falling down her cheeks
She kissed the picture she held in her hands
Bent over in grief, she softly spoke,

"Lord! It seems like yesterday
That I held my bundle of joy in my arms
As I watched her suckling my breast,
Her beautiful brown eyes staring into my face"

"So innocent,
Sweet,
Beautiful, and mine"

"Before I knew it,
My baby girl was all grown up.
No more pigtails, shoes, and socks
Now strutting high-heel shoes and hair flowing loose.
A graceful young woman
Walking down the aisle on college graduation day"

"My pride, my joy,
My baby girl, a brilliant rising star.
She was going to be big time"

"Not knowing the devil had a plan to take her out
When one day sickness took her down,
Like a wilted flower in bed, she lay
As we prayed to God to make her well"

"Every possible moment of my day,
I stayed beside her
Until one day, angels bore my baby girl
To heaven from whence she came."

In anger I asked God,

"Tell me why?
Why?
Why my baby girl had to die?"
She was mine, you gave her to me.
You could have taken me instead.
I have enjoyed a young life and am ready to go at any time.
But my baby girl was so young
Why! Why did you take her from me?"

No echoing response I heard
In self-pity, I hung my head

Welcoming solace from Satan
When he gave me all the things he had in stock
That momentarily closed my heart
From the grief and pain of my loss

Each day my tears of hurt like a fountain sprung
My heart in broken pieces clung
Its window I silently closed, locking out everyone
I was no longer me
When in depression, I sunk

I was selfish
Locked away in myself
Nothing human or inanimate mattered
Except my feelings of hurt from losing my baby girl

Until one day I heard the voice of an angel
In my ear whisper
Dry your tears mama
Let God and joy back in your life.
In heaven, I am waiting for you.

In humility I bowed, and to God I turned
To seek saving grace and healing of my broken self

Bless the Lord

Bless the lord for all his goodness
We could have lost our tongue in many ways
That made us unable to communicate

Bless the Lord for seeing eyes
To behold the glory of each day;
We could have been blind and never see it

Bless the Lord for a safe dwelling
With a bed to put our head;
We could have been homeless instead

Bless the Lord for clothes
That covers and protects our body;
We could have been naked as the day born

Bless the Lord for children, whether good or bad, behaving
They were given as gifts;
We could have had none to speak about

Bless the Lord for freedom to worship him;
We could have been banded from serving God
If there was not freedom of worship

Bless the Lord for food and drink on our table
Our daily bread that is always available;
We could have been improvised and be hungry

Bless the Lord for our family and friends
That cares all year round;
We could have been abandoned and lonely

Bless the Lord for our feet and hands
To be as independent as two hands and feet allows;
We could have lost them in war, accidents, and illness

Bless the Lord from our soul
For all these blessings he bestows
And for those that each day unfolds

No Tears in Heaven

I dreamed I had gone to the city
Where God, saints, and angels live
In a place called heaven

A whole new world of splendor and glory
Lit up, not by the sun, moon, stars, or electricity,
But by the countenance of God

Amazing heavenology allowed me to see
Everyone everywhere at one glance,
Including God

People of all nations and race,
Through heaven's door, arrive
Joyfully greeted by angels standing there

And a sign that read, "No tears in heaven.
We do not do it here in our haven."
Singing and praising our savior is what we do instead

Make Me Well

Lord, hear my cry
From the bottom of my belly
To the top of my voice
Heal my broken body
Make me well

Cure my illness
Keep me out of the grave
I can do nothing in there
I will be but dust

I want to stay alive
There is much to do here
That I can do

Hear my cry
Turn my sadness into joy
Do not ignore me, please

I will give thanks to thee
Morning noon and night
I will never be silent
With my wings soaring free

Imagine!

Imagine what it would be like
If, in heaven, we meet
The savior so sweet
United with families and friends
What a glory hallelujah dance
With angel wings flying free with no worries,
sad stories,
sickness,
physical, mental, and psychological abuse,
bullying,
claims,
crimes,
grim faces,
tears,
fears,
criticisms,
racism,
different languages,
grudges,
wickedness,
threats,
deaths,
etc., etc.
Just glory hallelujah and praises to a King
That lifted us out of miseries to a palace
To dance and sing
Imagine no stress!

Who Is This Man?

Who is this man that I see in the streets?
With knotted hair and tangled beard
His eyes downcast except for when he begs for change.

Who is this man that sits on the sidewalk?
In tattered clothing and rank odor
Surrounded by buzzing flies, stray cats, and dogs

Who is this man in the scorching summer heat?
With sunken eyes, cracked lips, and dry skin
With no water to quench his thirst

Who is this man in the cold winter's day?
Curled up against a wall fast asleep
Without a coat, scarf, gloves, or warm blanket

Who is this man who drags his feet?
Loaded down with filthy paper cups and plastic bags
Filled with newspaper and food from garbage bins

Who is this man I see standing against a graffiti wall?
At midday, yawning, exposing a mouth full of rotted teeth,
Trying to tie laces over his swollen feet with swollen hands

This man is one of God's children, just like you and me
Someone special that lost his way in life
Perhaps from life's struggles, war, or sickness
We may never know

This man in the street could be you,
A lost family member, friend, or sick soul,
And perhaps an angel in disguise

My Soul, Where Are You?

My soul
Where are you?

I am within you
The living part of you
The breath of life

I am your soul
I am you

Who Is This Woman?

Who is this woman?
Curled up against the subway walls
Surrounded by paper cups filled with cigarette butts
With tangled and dirt-matted hair
Hanging over her face and down her back

Who is this woman?
Laying on the sidewalk
Covered with debris and insect bites
Fast asleep, a ripped knapsack at her feet

Who is this woman?
Eyes unfocused, thick with crust
From tears that never touched the ground,
Her hands holding up a piece of cardboard box
Begging for help

Who is this woman?
On a park bench lay
Heedless of the sun, snow, or rain
Seasoned to homelessness and hopelessness

Who is this woman?
When hunger and thirst grips her in the guts,
Kills her pride and for food digs in a garbage bin

Who is this woman?
That forgets who she is
When from street to street
She drags her swollen feet
Looking for daily bread
And a place to lay her head

This woman could be me, you, or yours
That met upon hard times, illness, and more
A child of God who needs a helping hand
From a stranger who cares
If she lives or dies

You Are Healed

Weeping and moaning,
Calling upon God to help me
When angel music filled my room
And a hand was placed upon my head
I looked and saw no one

In my heart, I knew
The hand was that of God
The remedy in his clasp
To heal my broken parts

"Thank you, Lord," I shouted!
"For the touch of your hand!"
He responded in my heart
Weep no more, my child.
You are healed.

I Am God

I am God, the breath of life
Without which you cannot survive

I made the universe
At the blink of my eye
I can destroy it
Recreate it
Modify it
Exit it
Because I am God with the plan

I created all creatures, angels, and humans
Above and higher, below, and lower
I can destroy them
Recreate them
Alter them
Because I am God with their statistics

I am God
There is no other before or after me
To serve any imitation of me is to be foolhardy
Because that other is my creation

Who Are These Children?

Who are these children?
That sit on the banks of roadsides,
Dark alleys, lanes, and busy streets
Dirty and ragged, carrying book bags stuffed with rags
Wearing shoes without bottoms,
Their feet cracked, bleeding, and sore

Who are these children?
That stop vehicles on the streets
Begging for something to eat

Who are these children?
That gather nuts in the parks
Like squirrels we feed
Then, like groundhogs, they burrow
In holes and bushes to sleep

Who are these children?
That live in the cars of trains,
Buses, and abandon places,
Salvaging food from fast-food garbage bins

Who are these children?
That stand in the rain
Hoping to wash away bad stench,
Drying themselves
By the sun when it comes out

These children may be orphans,
Foster care runaways,
Abused, pedophile molested,
Lost, or bad behaving
On a homeless ride
Sometimes rescued by an angel

Sing Me a Song

Sing me a song
When you are sad

Sing me a song when you are happy
When with joy you are flying high

Sing me a song from your heart
Tell me what is going on

Sing me a song, no matter the tune
Sing me a song any way you can

Sing me a song
Even if the notes are wrong

Sing me a song
During rain or sunshine

Sing me a song
Any day and anytime

Sing me a song
No matter what you are doing

Sing me a song
So long as you have a voice

Sing me a song
All day if you can

Sing me a song
I am your King
I am always listening

Because He Cares

When, in your life's journey,
You come upon dark streets
Unable to see your way,
God appears a shining light
To help you on your path
Because he cares

When it seems you have hit the bottom of a pit,
God reaches down and lifts you up
Because he cares

Hopelessly lost in a desert,
God leaves you his footprints to follow
Because he cares

Saddened with a bleak day ahead,
God sends an angel to cheer you up,
Giving you hope to break out with a smile
Because he cares

Out on a storm-tossed sea,
God reaches out and calms your fears
Bringing you safely back to shore
Because he cares

Problems raining on your head,
God sends you a rainbow
To remind you he cares

Lonely with no one to keep you company,
God's presence is more than enough
Because he cares

Someone dislikes you,
God's great and everlasting love surrounds you
Because he cares

In the middle of wars and unrest,
God gives you peace
Because he cares

You Never Have to Worry

You never have to worry
if Jesus you have met
And in your heart he is kept

You never have to worry
if Jesus's words and path you follow;
He is the way, the truth, and life

You never have to worry
if to Jesus you want to speak;
He answers even before you call, and by his own time

You never have to worry
if you do not know what path to take;
Jesus is the greatest guide

You never have to worry
if your family ignores you;
Jesus is your father who art in heaven

You never have to worry
if your house forecloses;
When one door closes, Jesus opens another

You never have to worry
if you fall sick;
Jesus is a great physician and healer

You never have to worry
when things seem impossible;
Jesus makes all things possible

You never have to worry
which way to turn or go;
Jesus is the way, the truth, and life

You never have to worry
if you are in Jesus's plan;
He keeps it current all day long

The Collector

The devil is a collector
He always wants people
Good, bad, black, and white
He leads them into darkness
Their souls he keeps
In the valley of evil

Blinded, they walk in his presence
That only God can remove them from
When he opens their eyes to his saving grace

The Great Baptism

Colorful birds converged high and low
On trees above where the Jordan river flows

Forest and domestic animals hunched down
On stones and shrubs by the river's bank
Quietly, in anticipation of what happens next

Gentle breezes set wildflower petals swaying in the air
The sun, no less immune, shines from the sky

Man and nature stood still to witness a prophecy
Fulfilled when the water rippled like silver rings
When Jesus stepped in

God descended as a dove
A sign from above
To bless his son with reverence and love
As John baptized him

Bless the Stress Out

When you are stressed
To the point of distress,
Wishing to unwind
Right out of your mind,
Humbly bless the Lord for all things
Great and wonderful

That is, you, your family, and friends
The presence of all creatures
Treasured under the sun
Caged or on the run, some flying above

The love God pours on you that lifts you
When you are down

The beauty of nature he created
To calm and soothe you

The presence of changing seasons
Summer, Autumn, Winter, and Spring
That gives you no reasons
To doubt there is someone
Greater than anyone that lives on the earth

Fill your heart with all this
Leave no space for stress

A Mother's Keepsake

Mother, dear Mother,
Open your eyes
I am holding your hand
So cold, oh! So cold
I need to hear you call my name
Do not scare me so

Darling child,
I cannot be humanly aroused
An angel bore me home in the night
To the city of lights to be with my God

So please understand,
It was not my wish to leave like this
Without a goodbye or a kiss

Be comforted by the keepsakes
I gave you from birth

My arms that hugged you so many years
With love to greet or calm your fears

My ears that listened to your voice
In idle chatter and serious choices

My arms that held you from the day of your birth
Until my departure from earth

My God I shared with you
In preparation for a day like this

Our memories you must keep
For I am now out of your reach

Stay safe and well until again we meet
Never to part company again

The Messiah

Many years before Jesus became a baby
in the womb of a virgin maiden,
Royal families, prophets, priests, and peasants
talked about him until the day of his arrival

When he was birthed by Mary the lowly maiden,
Not by a princess or queen,
In a stable, not a palace or inn,
Sleeping in a manger, not a crib

A monumental surprise for the rich and famous,
Including the Scribes, Pharisees, and Sadducees

A welcome from simple shepherds
That located and worshipped him

A great expectation from foreign wise men
That searched, found, and honored him

The fulfillment of scriptures for Simeon
And the prophetess Anna in the temple

A threat to nervous royal kingdoms
That attempted to assassinate him at birth

Acknowledged by God by the signal of a white dove
When John the Baptist, his forerunner, baptized him

Tracked, observed, and harassed by the Scribes and Pharisees
When he toured Jerusalem accompanied by the city's finest men
Among throngs of people who followed him

He attracted the mighty, the powerful,
The cynical, the wise, the foolish, the rich, and the poor
He listened, he reasoned, but never argued

He discredited evil priests and kings
In retaliation and fear, they bought him
For thirty pieces of silver

In the garden of Gethsemane, his place of prayer,
An angel strengthened him before they took him
On a donkey back through the streets of Jerusalem

Like a king, they thronged him
Like a criminal, they tried him
Like a thief, they crucified him
A murder still unmatched

In his friend's tomb, they buried him
Three days later, he walked out of it
Provided proof to those who doubted him
And gave hope to those who followed him

The Eyes of Poverty

On a cold winter day, and a little heat in a small house,
A little baby boy dressed in summer clothes and bare feet
Screamed for his mama, and she picked him up

"What is wrong my precious?
Mama is right here for you,"
With weary arms and calloused hands,
To her breast she brought him
Hungrily, he suckled until he fell asleep

She went back into the kitchen
And stared at the stack of dirty dishes in the sink
Beneath a broken faucet leaked
Tired, she sat down and fell asleep at the kitchen table

In the late hours of the night she heard her children crying,
Huddled together to keep warm,
Too hungry to play or complain
In the late hours of the night
Had gathered around their papa's photo

She gathered them into her arms and whispered,
"Do not cry my children,
I can hear your daddy's wings.
It is a signal we are not alone.
Let us pray like we did when he was here with us."

Together mother and children prayed
Then went to bed huddled close

The next morning there was a knock on their door
God had sent them warm clothes and food
And a plumber to fix the faucet

Upon the Wings of the Wind

When dark clouds in your life pop up

Raining hailstones, thunder, and lightning,

Distress and stress signs glaring at you

Just waiting to conquer and destroy

The happiness in your life,

Do not panic!

Ride the wings of the angels of God

Full of glory and grace

That will fly you out of all of this

Into shining light with a joyful smile

The Church on the Mountain

The giant rocky mountain
Cradled the little church in its crescent arms
Surrounded by huge rocks, sparse grass,
And graveled bed, overlooking a valley
Of vegetation, fruit trees, and wood cottages

There was no electricity
Spirit lanterns lit the church
The seats were long wood benches,
And its windows had no panes of glass

Sunday school was held inside and outside
On rocky ground and beneath dry trees
Memorizing and reciting scriptures
From the books of the Holy Bible

Come Sunday morning, the pews were filled
With everyone that knew each other
It was one big family of Christians and sinners
Worshipping God on that mountain top

From the old piano, in a corner of the pew,
Music flowed and voices sung
"To the old rugged cross, I will ever be true."

Redemption songs would echo from the mountain
Stopping people in their path to pause
And sometimes come into the church

This is the church where I fell in love
With Jesus, and he accepted me
And I married him with no regrets

My Jesus, I Thank You

My Jesus, I thank you
For standing up for me
You could have denied your heritage
As the son of God
Instead you took up that significant wooden cross
On which you were nailed at Mount Calvary
A punishment for a crime you did not commit,
Bearing the shame of a criminal you were not
Innocent of any evil act
Chosen by your father in heaven
To save your people from their sins
Like a lamb to your slaughter when you did

Alive and About

The sun broke through the sky
Its brilliant radiance dispelled the dawn
To greet a group of sad-faced women
Stealthily walking in the streets
Of a city not yet fully awake

They entered the Garden of Joseph
The flower blossoms slowly awakening
As they pulled out spices and ointments
From beneath their cloaks,
Eyes darting all over in fear of being found out

The creeper-clad rock with the stone door was wide open
Admitting the pious women's scrutiny,
Expectantly looking for Jesus
But found only his linen wraps

Frightened, they ran outside and bumped
Into an angel who told them,
"Jesus is not resting there anymore."

Amazed, they ran to his disciples in mourning
With the good news that Jesus was up and about

Trouble

Trouble has been around since
God made Adam and Eve
And kicked Satan out of heaven's reach

It is an unwelcome visitor
That sneaks in or openly walks into your life
Any time of day or night,
Sleeping or awake

It does not matter who you are
Sometimes it sits for a short while
Or linger for a long time

Sometimes it comes to visit in twos
Or behind each other, depending on how it starts
And those involved

To get rid of trouble is always a battle
Especially if you do not know the cause
Or the reason it came to visit

Some people see trouble fast asleep
And wake it up just for a laugh or out of spite
This is never a good idea because trouble
Is trouble and never a good friend

If you are not a believer in the Christian faith,
Then trouble you will not know how to defeat
Without the tools to destroy it

Trouble knows the easy people in its reach,
But the sanctified and holy baptized,
It thinks twice before it hits

Because the holy spirit burns out carnal nature
The name of trouble when disguised

So when trouble visits, it is best to call
On God to deliver you
Before it wins and takes you out

The Holy Ghost Mission

When the Holy Ghost is on a mission
To fulfill a promise made,
It picks up steady speed and, like a mighty wind,
Descends on you

Stirring you to move to the beat of his spirit
To fulfill God's plan for you

Sometimes he lets you dance all night
To enjoy the glory he brings in your life

Sometimes he lets you pray a long time,
Tarrying for a purpose until God gives a breakthrough

Sometimes he lets you lay your hands on people
To see him work a miracle

Sometimes he opens your mouth to prophesy
To open the eyes of the blind and the ears of the deaf

Sometimes he takes you on a ride down a river
To experience peace like the water as it flows

Sometimes he lights a fire to catch the eyes of others
To experience a burning spirit to keep them hot

Sometimes it is a call you must answer
To do God's will in your life

The Holy Ghost is a giver, not a taker
A gift from God to those who accept him

Thirty Years of Ministry

Jesus, a special loan from heaven
His birth foretold in Genesis
Happened on a cold winter night
Where shepherds and angels mingled
And wise men appeared
Bringing tokens to worship him

In the temple, at age twelve,
He aggravated the priests with his wisdom
Then left them to ponder on his words
And stayed out of sight
Until John the Baptist baptized him
In the River Jordan

In the Judaean Desert, he fasted
And was tempted by the devil that left in a huff
When he ran him off and angels came to minister to him

To Jerusalem he journeyed
And recruited twelve men to follow him,
Ministering to people in valleys, mountains,
Plains, and by the seashore
Healing the sick, resurrecting the dead,
Giving sight to the blind,
Kicking demons back to hell

His journeys took him in the path of scorners,
Haters, rich publicans, and good Samaritans
Some converted to his teachings,
Supporting him quietly until his death

Many women, some with questionable pasts,
Loved and followed him; some stood afar off,
Worshipping him

In Bethany, the Holy Ghost anointed him
When a strange woman poured
Perfume upon his head from an alabaster jar

A triumphal entry on a donkey's back
Into Jerusalem to the temple, he went
Declaring his holy royal status
That angered indignant unbelievers
To throw him out with angry shouts

Ignoring of their outbursts, he attended his last supper
From there to the garden of Gethsemane to pray
He was arrested, taken, and court-sentenced to death
On the hill of Golgotha, he was murdered by crucifixion
In the tomb of Joseph of Arimathea, his body was laid
On the third day he walked out, leaving his clothes behind
He did not need it anymore; he was headed for higher grounds,

On the Mount of Olives, he met his eleven disciples
With the promise of the Holy Ghost and Pentecost
He said goodbye and walked away

Airborne in a silent wind, he went to heaven

Salvation

Salvation from God is a mighty rock
The solid ground on which you stand
It cannot be moved or pushed;
It is steadfast and sure,
Rooted in God's holy ground
Covered by the Holy Ghost
Surrounded by holy angels
That never grow old

The Christmas Angel's Message

In the small village of Nazareth
The Christmas Angel flew

A humble and poor maiden
Heard the rustling of an angel's wings

He was standing in front of her
His stance indicated he was not just passing by

With fear in her heart,
She listened to the heavenly being
Deliver the message from his King

Surprised at the message,
She responded,

"It is an incredible honor, sir,
But I fear you are mistaken because
I live with my humble folks and am
Soon to be married to a village carpenter."

"Oh! Mary, I am not mistaken.
God has made you his choice,"
Was the angel's response

Concerning the coming of the Messiah,
Mary was not ignorant of the prophecies
She just did not expect to be his chosen mother

Gracefully and humbly
In obedience to God,
She accepted the message

Communication Line to Glory

Jesus is on call anytime
There are no restrictions to his calls
His line is always open to the world
The bill was paid forever at Mount Calvary

His line is a lifeline
He treats all calls as emergencies
Never can it be tampered with
Out of service, disconnected, or interrupted

Guarded by angels,
Provided with power from grace,
It takes only the dials of faith
For him to respond according to your needs

Jesus, The Light of Life

A world in darkness once was
Until God created the sun, moon, and stars

An unborn life in darkness lives
Until from its mother's womb it comes to behold light

A blind person in darkness lives
With an inner light only he sees

A sinner in darkness lives
Until God forgives him of his sins

Come Home

Oh! Tired soul
Stressed and depressed by sin
Come home to Jesus
Be washed and made clean
From sin, be set loose
From bondage to freedom
This is how God works

Protect Me, Lord

Lord, when my enemies and my foes
In the secret or in the light
Seek me day and night
Surrounding me like hungry bears,
Slithering snakes, and sticky porcupines
Seeking to hurt me because of strife,
Jealousy, or pure hatred,
Or for no apparent cause

Protect me with your mighty power
Keep me from falling in their snares
Set to conquer my body, soul, and spirit

Lift me over the pits they dig
Take me out of the fires they start
Be my lifejacket when in deep waters I am thrown

Protect my daily bread
Let it not be taken out of my mouth

Let mine enemies not have any victory
When they try to harm me

Let me overcome their evil with good
When under your wings I seek shelter
From their plans for me

Hard Rocks

Hard rocks from unexpected places
Strike like a lightning bolt
When friends become snakes
Slithering out of holes and crevices
To expose themselves as foes

When those for whom you care
Turn their backs on you,
Forgetting the kindness to them you showed
When things with them were down to naught

Not forgetting your enemies that lurk
In unexpected places to touch you if they can
Planning day and night how to throw hard rocks
To knock you out of sight

Do not be dismayed at all these hard rocks
Lean on God, the rock of your salvation
That gives you faith and grace to cover you
From all the rocks that are thrown at you

Joy!

Joy!
Real joy!
Wonderful joy!
Long-lasting joy!
Always available from Jesus in heaven
That gives it away for free
To anyone who asks
Believing by faith

Broken Pieces

I was broken earthenware
When God gathered my pieces
From off a discarded heap of broken wares

With gentle care, he washed my pieces,
Soaked me in his precious blood;
Like clay I once more became

Then he placed me upon his potter's wheel,
Molded me according to his design
A refined and redefined vessel I became
That was glazed and fired and removed from his kiln

Filled with the Holy Ghost
A shiny new me for God to use
When, with steady hands, he signed his signature
Claiming me as his own

Keep Your Eyes Upon the Cross

Keep your eyes upon the cross
Your feet on Mount Calvary
Your hands before you clasped
Never wavering or faltering
Never doubting or arguing

The salvation of Jesus
The price he paid for man
The victory claimed
When from the grave he arose
To ascend into heaven
Where he lives today,
The crowned prince of glory

The lamb for sinners slain
That shall one day return to earth
At a time unknown
To claim the good, not the bad
To return to glory,
The home of the saved

Lord! Hear Our Cry

Lord! Hear our cry!
From earth beyond the sky
To heaven listen up
We need your angels at our side
During these troublesome times
Of stress from crimes,
Escalated hate, and pain in every nation
Causing wars and rumors of wars,
Ration of foods, national insecurities,
And the cruelties of terrorism
That is causing fear in every heart

Satan is in a vile rage
It can be heard and seen
Like a movie on a screen
Creating a rampage on land and sea
From valleys to mountains
In the deserts and the plains

Cripple his army, oh! Lord!
Let your power override
His plans for us
Give us guidance to reach out to those
He has plans to recruit

Do not let them fall blindly in his trap
Open their eyes and minds that are tightly closed
Help them to make the right decision whom to serve.

My Jesus, I Love You

My Jesus, I love you
For coming to earth as an innocent child
Humble and amazing,
Setting an example for children to follow

My Jesus, I love you
For being a young man
So holy and obedient
To your father in heaven
When you gave your life for all

My Jesus, I love you
For the disciples you left behind
To teach Christianity according to your words
To those who want to learn

My Jesus, I love you,
For ignoring
Satan in the wilderness
When he attempted to tempt you
To abandon the purpose for which you came

My Jesus, I love you
For healing the sick and disabled
For feeding the hungry and forsaken
Setting the example for us to follow

My Jesus, I love you
For your tolerance and demeanor
In addressing the anger and rage
Of the ignorant crowds that terrorized you

My Jesus, I love you
For admitting your kinship with God
When, through the streets of Jerusalem, you walked,
Carrying your cross to Golgotha
Among the jeers of an ignorant people

My Jesus, I love you
For giving up your life
A sacrifice for all mankind;
The only one of its kind

My Jesus, I love you
For setting aside the mighty rock
Like a feather when out of your sepulcher
A radiant light, you stepped outside
Your mission accomplished
A living proof of who you are
When from earth to heaven you ascended
Leaving behind the Holy Ghost to keep us company

The Feet of Jesus

Holy feet to the temple they walked
To set wrong things right
Fulfilling prophecy everywhere he went

On mountains, in valleys, and plains
Stepping on dirt, desert sand, pebbles, and stones,
Never once complaining of the distance he walked
Though weary and tired his feet must have been

On the sea he walked,
Not an apparition
That Peter and his other disciples saw,
But the son of God

Mary of Bethany in gratitude
For raising her kin Lazarus
With a pound of spikenard
Anointed his feet with thanks

Mount Olivet, he climbed with ease
In the wilderness, he walked
In the Garden of Gethsemane, he went to pray
His travels all over the city about to end

Through Jerusalem Street, he rode
The King of all kings to Golgotha to be killed
His final footsteps on tired feet
Nailed to a cross, a holy masterpiece

The Lord Is My Life

The Lord is my vision, night and day
I depend on him to lead me in the right way

He is my strength; I fear no fall
When evil upon my doorsteps land
Or in my path stand

I will not run nor will my heart fail
Because it cannot touch any part of me

I will, with confidence, stand firm,
For I serve a living God
That hears and knows my voice

When I call on him, soft or loud
The signal of wings I hear
Coming my way

Why Worry About Today

Do not worry about today
No matter what the day brings;
Worry cannot change a thing

Do not worry about yesterday
It is forever gone,
Archived in the past
It cannot be retrieved
By any thought or human action
To be corrected, changed, or undone

Do not worry about tomorrow
As to what kind of day it will be
Today is a new day
That God has allowed you to greet
Make it the best day ever
After yesterday and before tomorrow

The Lord Is My Leader

The Lord is my leader
Each day I follow him
In the path he leads

When I grow weary,
I fall at his feet
He restores my faith,
Gives me strength

Even when in the shadow of death,
I meet in valleys, mountains, and plains

His goodness and mercies
Are bestowed on me
Enough to walk the path

We Dare Not Walk Alone

In this world filled with love and hate,
We dare not walk without faith.
Secured by the blood of the lamb
Shed for you and me
To safely walk day and night
Under God's wings of love

To ward off Satan's strategies
Perpetuated with strong energies
To deceive, ensnare, and trick us into serving him

But if resilient against sin we stand,
With God leading us by the hand,
We will this life endure
In peace and love secure
To God's glory forevermore

Why Do I Need Jesus?

"Why do I need Jesus?" argued the professor
"He is just a significant person
Like the Pope, Martin Luther King Jr.,
Prophets, and others like them.
Why the big ahem?
What can a dead man and his story do for me?"

He jumped in his car onto the highway,
A speeding vehicle swerved his way
"Have mercy on me Jesus!" he screamed!
The vehicle instantly came to a stop
"Thank you Jesus, thank you Jesus!" he whispered

When he got home, there was an urgent message
From his doctor to come in and see him
He did not hesitate and went to his doctor

The doctor looked at him with sadness, and he said,
"Your MRI results shows you have a brain tumor."

In shock, the professor shouted!
"Jesus living Christ! What am I going to do?
I need you! I need you!
More than ever I need you!"

He bowed his head, tears dripping to the ground
He left the doctor's office and went home

Someone had left a flyer on his doorknob that read
"Jesus is alive."
You spoke to him today,
He heard your cry,
He answered you,
He can meet all your needs
When on your knees you acknowledge him
And forgiveness of your sins seek

Down on his knees, he prayed aloud,
"Jesus, my Lord and savior,
You are alive, forgive my sins and unbelief.
Make me yours from this day forever."

God heard him and forgave his sins
And covered him with his wings

The Void

I get up in the morning
Filled with discontent,
Not from want of wealth
Or anything of consequence,
But from an emptiness
I could not fill or comprehend.
Searching each day for a remedy
Until one unforgettable day,
Thirsty and weary from my long quest,
I stumbled and fell at Jesus's feet
He took possession of my soul,
Filling the void in me

Breaking Free

There are some things in life
We hold onto or that holds onto us
From which we need to let go,
Breaking free to be free

Perhaps from an idol
You favor above God

Perhaps a friendship or relationship
That keeps you out of God's reach

Perhaps it's sour grapes
That its taste will not disappear

Perhaps it's childhood hurts
That in your heart lurks

Perhaps it is revenge you are planning
For someone that hurt you

Perhaps you have told lies
For which someone suffered or died

Perhaps it is a situation
You cannot speak about

That God can break every link one by one
If you ask him to break you free

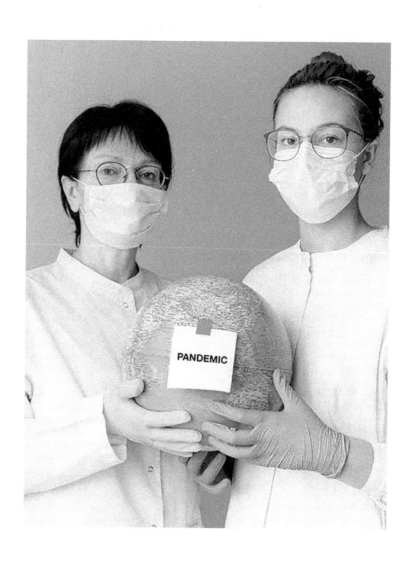

COVID-19

Like a mighty strong wind,
It flew in on strong wings
From somewhere to everywhere

From the unknown into light, it creeps
Into our eyes, nose, mouths, and hands
A sneeze, a hug, kiss, and handshake;
It sticks and cleaves and enters you

You may survive its entrance and residence,
Or if it is your time to exit the world,
It accompanies you

Its death toll has put the world on pause
To remind everyone God is in charge
And that we need his intervention
To pour out his mercy and still this storm
That has our nation in a pandemic

We must not be discouraged,
But pray for courage to face its trial
That is a fierce and strong foe
That cannot overthrow our God
His victory over COVID-19 is secure

Let us have faith along with hope
As we learn to cope with our fears and isolation
Our song should always be one of praise
Each day we greet a new morning
And hear birds sing and flowers bloom
It means we are blessed; God is watching over us

God of All

Amazing power of Jesus
Let angels and humans hail him, God of all
The sovereign crown that rules and saves us by his grace,
To him be glory and praise

My spirit yearns for thee to come close to me
Let me feel your presence, Lord
Speak your words to me
I will listen with all my heart
And keep them in my thoughts
To live a godly life

O My Soul

O my soul that has lost its sun
Wake up! Shake up and joyfully rise
be smart and do your part,
light up the dark in your heart

Shout out to God
he will rekindle your faith
and make your life shine again

Thank You, Jesus

Thank you, Jesus, for lifting me up
When I am down

Thank you, Jesus, for comforting me
When I mourn

Thank you, Jesus, for humility;
It has opened doors for me

Thank you, Jesus, for satisfying
My thirst after righteousness

Thank you, Jesus, for your mercy
When I mess up and you give me a second chance

Thank you, Jesus, for a clean heart,
An assurance that I will one day meet you

Thank you, Jesus, for peace
That brings relief from stress and my enemies

Thank you, Jesus, for the signal of wings;
May it make a difference in someone's life

If by reading the *Signal of Wings* a soul is saved,
Then to God be the Glory and praise

For one more space in heaven will be filled
A better place to one day be when from this life you leave.

The Signal

The wind and the waves
Like angels, they move
A distinct sound like a signal it makes
Touching everything and everyone in its path;
Ethereal and serene,
Unforgettable in each heart

The Lord Is Home

Out in the cold, a young man wandered
With a mountain on his back
On a rough and steep road
Looking for hope

In deep waters, he fell
Pitch black were his nights
And the valleys he passed through
Full of weeds, snakes, and debris
His hands and feet blistered and torn
Pierced by thistles and thorns

Unaware God was watching him
He came upon a path outlined with blood
And a cross at the end of the road

An angel echoed loud and clear
Come follow me, the Lord is home.
He will remove your mountain
And create a new heart within you.
Rejoice and be glad someone was praying for you.

A cry erupted from the young man
As he fell at the cross
"Thank you, Jesus, for bringing me to you.
I surrender, I surrender, I surrender.
Take my mountain and set me free,
It is too heavy to keep."

An Amazing Friend

We have a sovereign friend
We can tell him all our secrets and complaints

He attends our trials and temptations;
We never end up losing

When trouble comes our way,
He stands beside us and guides us out of it

When a love one passes,
He shares the sorrow and dries our tears

When we are weak and distressed,
He strengthens us and relieves our stress

When we are lonely and afraid,
He sends his angel to keep us company

When our enemies attack,
He covers us with his armor of righteousness,
And they back off

When we are broke,
He supplies our needs and wants

When we are low or down,
He lifts us up with faith and hope

When we fall,
He picks us up and puts us on a rock to stand

When we need to talk,
He gives us his undivided attention
And does not fall asleep

What greater friend can we have
When he is a sovereign king who gave his life for us
Our greatest hope is to meet him on his return to earth

Heaven Express

Heavens Airline Express Jet,
A magnificent sight
Its wings opened wide
Arriving like a thief in the night
On earth's airstrip for an outgoing flight

Passengers from all over the world
Checked in with empty hands
No shipped or overhead luggage;
They were delivered at calvary

Escorted by angel security, they boarded the jet
With passports, tickets, and IDs stamped with the blood of Jesus
And scanned in heaven for arrival

The moment they got in, an angel greeted them
With a golden smile that lit up the cabins
That were not segregated as first class or economy
The flight was equal opportunity; no class specification

"Welcome to Heavens Air Express
There are no seat belts, oxygen masks, drinks, or snacks,
Or turbulence, or bad weather expected
Captain Jesus is our pilot, the breath of life,
With the whole world in his hand."

The pilot guided the jet onto to the runway and into the sky
In the blink of an eye, he landed on heaven's runway
Amidst flashing stars and angels on standby

"We have landed,
Thank you for making heaven your destination
You may disembark through the open doors,"
The pilot announced

The passengers of all races and ages,
Rich and poor, healthy and sick
In golden silence exited the jet
And met the glory of heaven, King Jesus,
That changed their alien status to heaven's citizens

Their shouts of praises in one language
Through heaven rang,
A reunion and celebration about to begin

About the Author

Join Leonie Stair as she welcomes her debut book *the Signal of Wings*, a spiritual and inspirational thought-provoking book.

Leonie is a former teacher and graduate from Sam Sharpe Teachers' College, Jamaica, West Indies. A graduate of Herbert H. Lehman College and a licensed nursing home administrator.